Dino Detectives

Paul Mason

Contents

OXFORD
UNIVERSITY PRESS

 This page is for an adult to read to you.

Mini, Macro and Micro World!

Hello. My name is **Mini Marvel**. My dad **Macro Marvel** and I invented **Micro World**. This is the book that inspired us to make the **Forbidden Valley** zone.

My dad Macro Marvel

You are here

 This page is for an adult to read to you.

Did you know?

There are lots of different ways of measuring length, for example centimeters (cm) and metres (m). Look out for any measurements in this book.

Fact!

The largest Tyrannosaurus rex skeleton ever found was nicknamed Sue after the person who discovered it, Sue Hendrikson.

Mini's Top Spot

Can you find this caption in the book?

> This bone was found in South America in 2014.

Can you remember why we use captions?

 This page is for an adult to read with you.

Before you read

Sound checker

The sounds to remember when you are reading this book.

re our ear (w)or

Word alert

Blend the sounds. Remember the sounds you have practised.

centre labour heard work

Into the zone

What do you know about dinosaurs? Do you have a favourite dinosaur?

Clues to the past

A lot of what we know about dinosaurs comes from their bones. The bones can tell us about what different dinosaurs looked like, what they ate, and even what colour they were!

Bone hunters

Dino detectives search for bones inside rocks. Sometimes they have to dig deep into the earth to find the rocks.

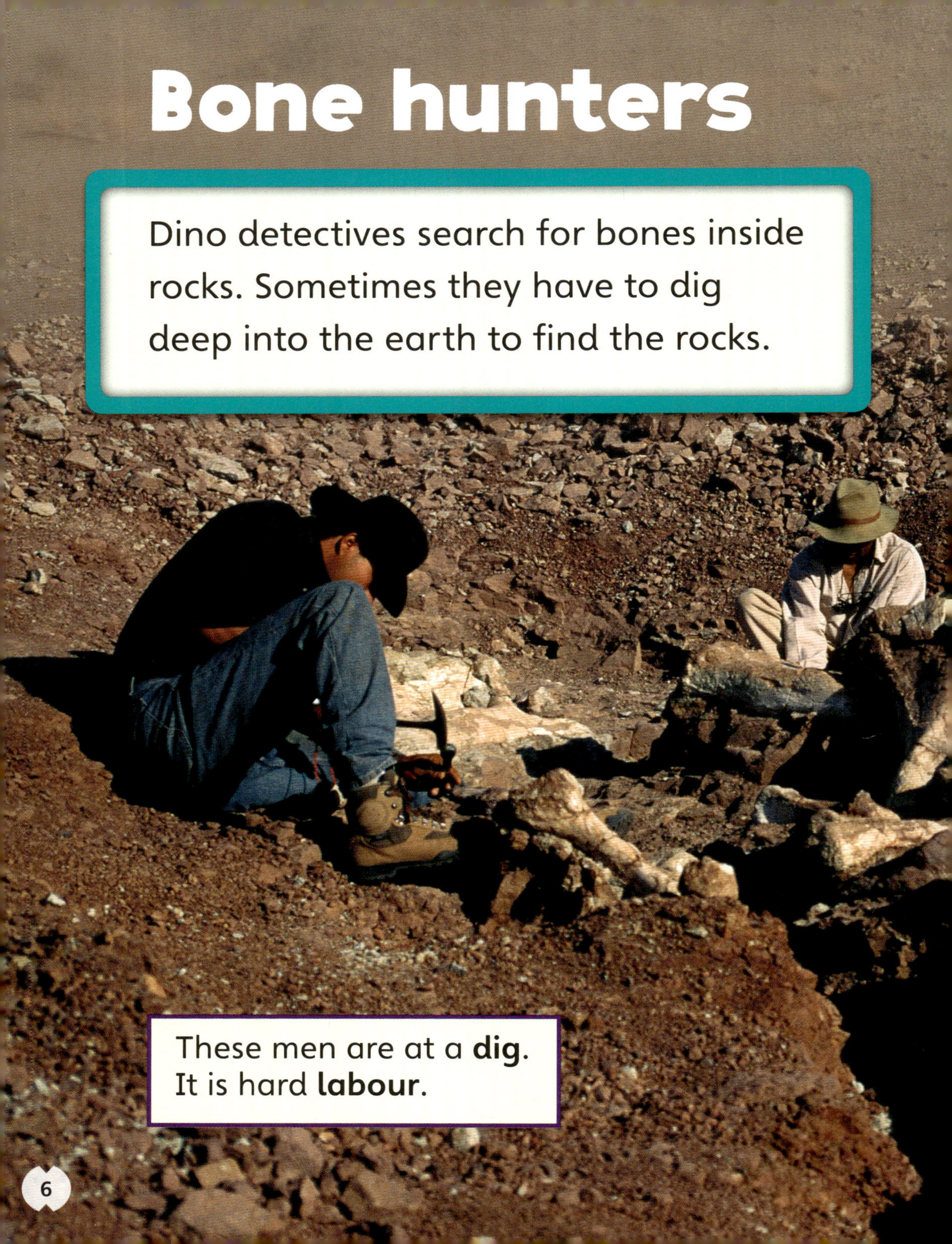

These men are at a **dig**. It is hard **labour**.

It's like a treasure hunt.
This rock has been split to reveal a dinosaur skeleton at the centre.

Living clues

Dino detectives are **eager** to learn as much about dinosaurs and their world as possible. The teeth of this dinosaur tell us that it was a meat eater.

This is what this dinosaur looked like. It had a hooked claw on each foot that it used to clamp down its victims.

sharp, pointed
teeth

Giant clues

Just one bone can help guide dino detectives. This bone is from the leg of an unknown dinosaur. By measuring the bone, dino detectives can work out how big the dinosaur was.

Experts think this dinosaur could have been the biggest creature that ever lived. They think it could have been 40 metres long and 20 metres tall!

This bone was found in South America in 2014.

A big bite!

This skeleton shows that *Tyrannosaurus rex* was a mighty **carnivore**! Its powerful jaws and sharp teeth could crunch through tough bone.

Swimming dinosaurs

Spinosaurus had a narrow head and straight teeth. Dino detectives think that *Spinosaurus* swam and hunted fish.

This is what dino detectives think *Spinosaurus* looked like.

Eyes ahead

First *Velociraptor* stared ...
then it attacked!

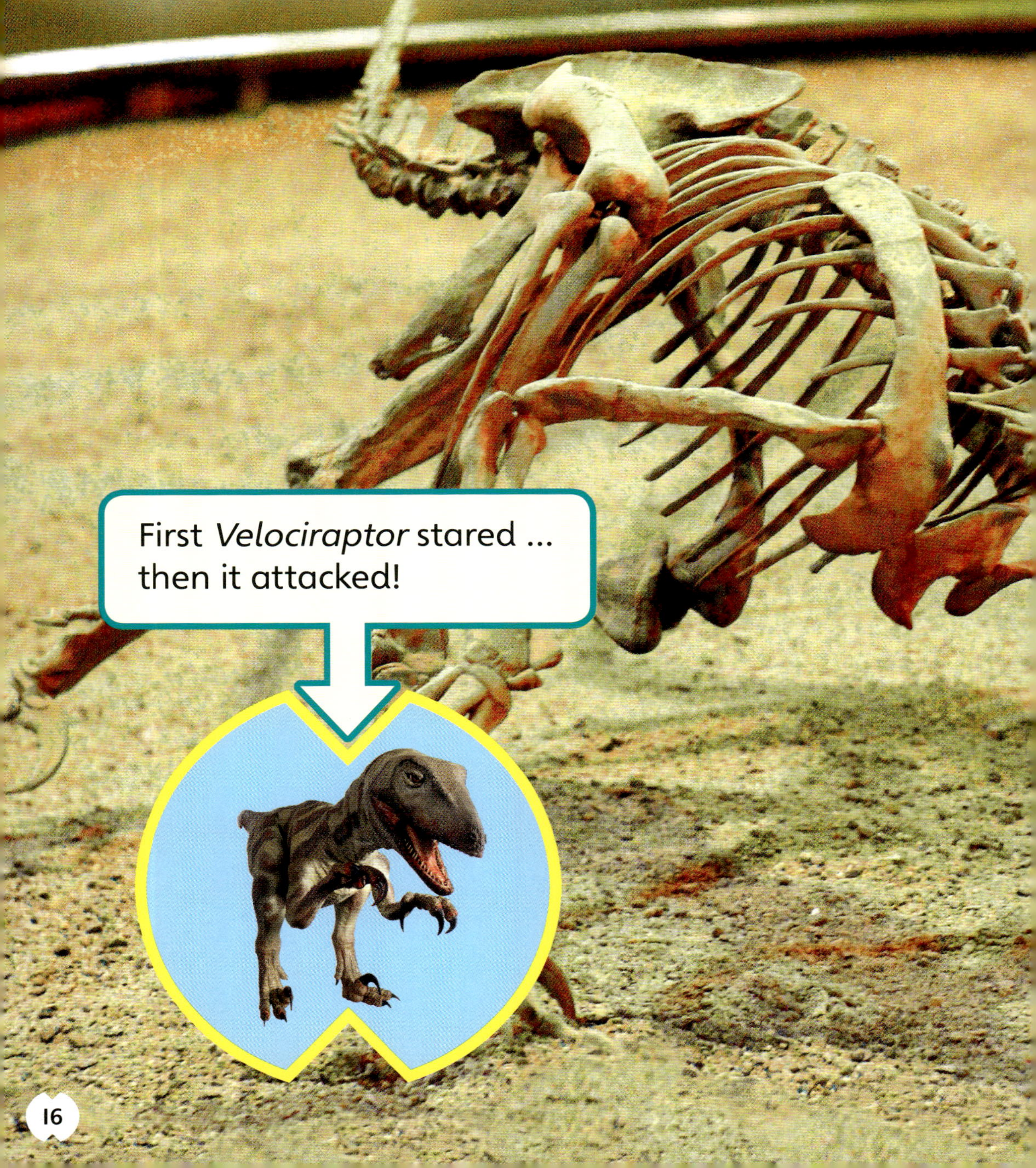

Predators' eyes often point straight ahead. They look straight towards the creature they want to catch. *Velociraptor's* skull shows it had the eyes of a predator.

Dinosaur noises

The tube on the head of this *Parasaurolophus* looks like a trombone! Dino detectives think it may have been used to make noises. Other dinosaurs in their pack heard the **eerie** signals.

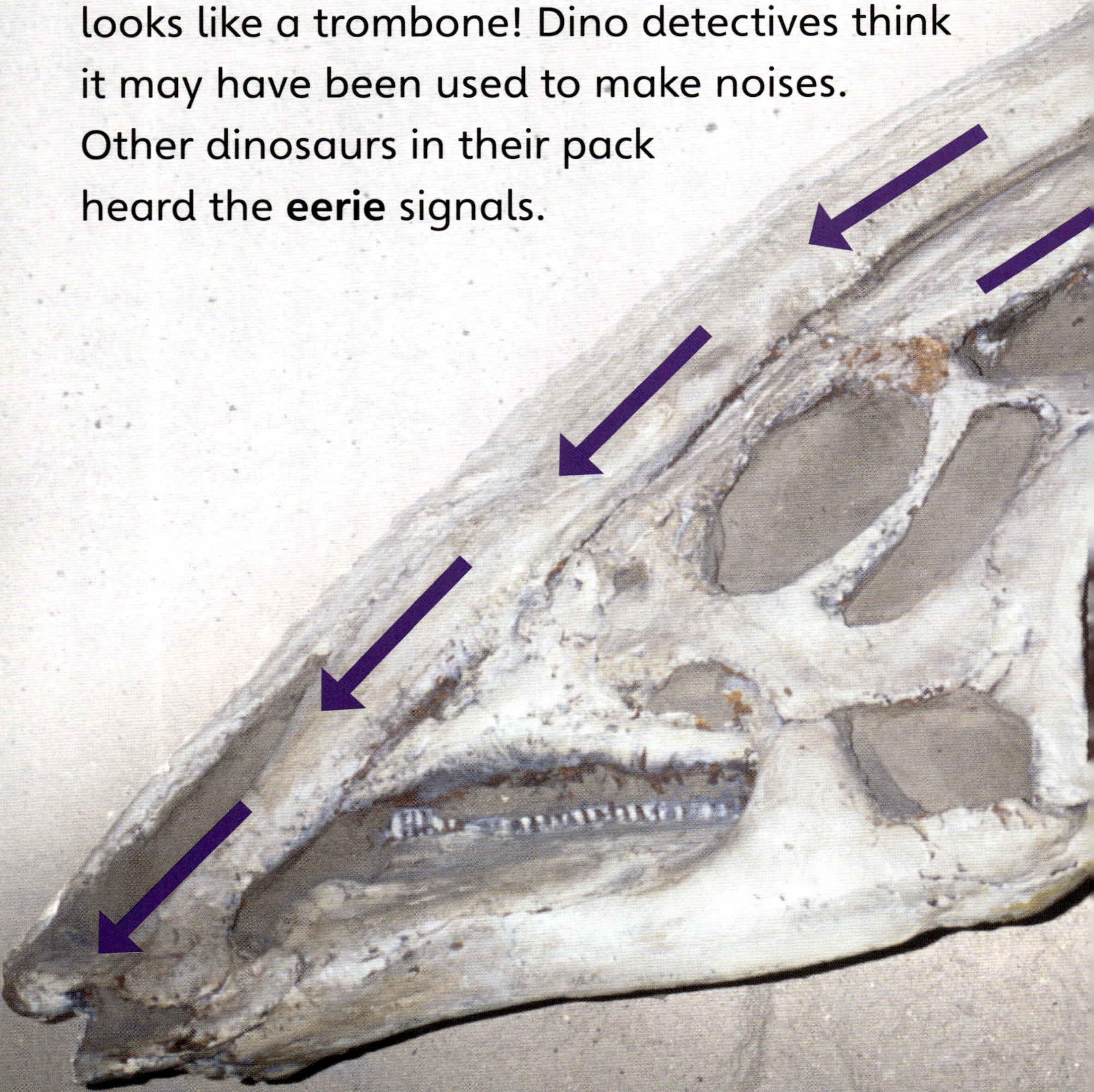

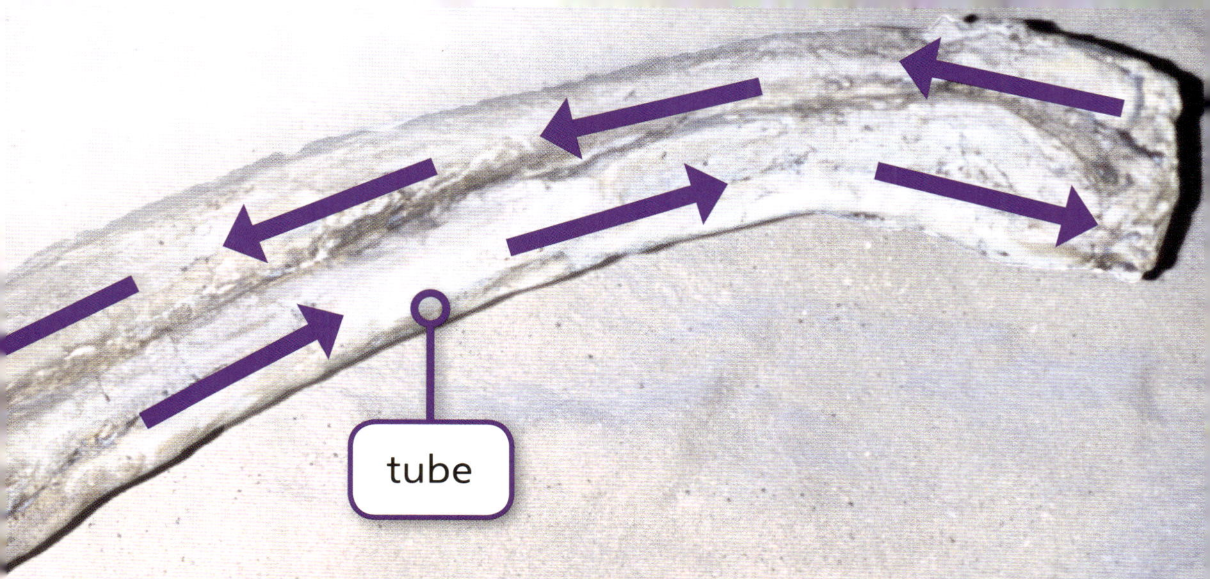

This is what the *Parasaurolophus* looked like.

Feathered reptiles

Dinosaurs were **reptiles** but dino detectives have discovered that some had feathers, like birds! This is *Microraptor*.

The long feathers helped *Microraptor* glide between trees.

long legs
arm feathers

Colour clues

Dino detectives test bones to try to work out what colour dinosaurs were. The shape of tiny structures in the **remains** can show what colour the feathers might have been.